Iceheart

By Joy Cowley

Illustrated by Francis Phillipps

⊕ Dominie Press, Inc.

Publisher: Christine Yuen
Editor: John S. F. Graham
Designer: Lois Stanfield
Illustrator: Francis Phillipps

Published by:

̃℗ Dominie Press, Inc.

1949 Kellogg Avenue
Carlsbad, California 92008 USA

www.dominie.com

Paperback ISBN 0-7685-1087-2
Library Bound Edition ISBN 0-7685-1531-9
Printed in Singapore by PH Productions Pte Ltd
  2 3 4 5 6 PH 04 03

Table of Contents

Chapter One
Gifts of the Winds

Long ago, in a faraway land, there was a king and queen who longed for a child. Years went by, and they had a fine baby boy. Oh, what rejoicing there was! Bells rang. People danced in the streets. At the palace, there was a huge party in the grand ballroom. Guests came from all over the world.

The four winds blew in, wearing their most beautiful clothes. Each carried a gift for the new prince.

The West Wind was dressed in all the

colors of the desert—red, orange, yellow, brown. Her gift was a chain with a small hummingbird made of jewels. "Wear this to fly," she said.

The South Wind's cloak was made of summer flowers. When she moved, the grand hall was filled with the scent of jasmine and ginger blossom. She put before the prince a golden music box. "Play this for sleep," she said.

The East Wind was dressed in silks the color of a peacock's tail. Her perfume was from the spices of Asia, and her gift for the prince was an emerald lamp. "Hold this for light," she said.

Then came the North Wind in a flurry of snow. Her robe was of white fur, and there were icicles in her hair. She carried a whistle made of ivory. "Blow this for a blizzard," she said. She bent over to lay the whistle by the prince's cot, but the spicy perfume of the East Wind made her sneeze. Such a sneeze it was! Her cold breath blew through the grand ballroom and cracked wine glasses. It frosted mirrors. But that damage was not the worst.

The heart of the baby prince was turned to ice.

Chapter Two

Happiness is Only a Word

Young prince Tashka grew strong and clever. He could ride a horse bareback. At a hundred paces, he could fire an arrow over his shoulder and split a bamboo cane. It was said he could wrestle dragons all day and not get tired.

He was also very handsome. His hair was as black as coal, and his eyes were as blue as the inside of an iceberg. Yet as soon as people met him, they knew there was something missing. The prince showed no emotion. The ice in his heart had not affected his strength, but his feelings were frozen and dead.

"Are you happy, son?" the king asked.

"I don't know what you mean," the boy replied.

"You must know what happiness is," the king insisted.

"It is only a word," said the prince.

The queen asked him, "Dear son, do you love us?"

"Tell me what love is," he answered.

So it was, that the prince grew to manhood, knowing neither love nor hate, neither happiness nor sadness. Everyone in the land called him Prince Iceheart, and because the prince had no emotion, he didn't mind the name at all.

Chapter Three

Cold Through
and Through

When Prince Tashka was old enough to marry, the king and queen sent a message throughout the land. Any woman who could make the prince fall in love would be his bride.

The most beautiful women came from far and wide. They sang and danced for the prince. They showered him with sweet talk and kisses. They brought him gifts of horses and swords and fine suits of armor. But nothing they said or did could make him fall in love.

"He is cold through and through," said one.

"He is truly Iceheart," said another.

One by one, the beautiful women went away to seek other men who knew how to laugh and love.

Now, there was a servant in the palace who had a daughter called Serena. She was the same age as the prince. She was not rich. Her face was not beautiful. But she had a quick wit and a warm, loving heart that made her eyes glow. Serena was kind to everyone, and she was especially fond of the prince, whom she had known all her life.

She said to her father, the palace servant, "What a pity Prince Tashka cannot fall in love with one of those fine young women. There must be some way of melting the ice in his heart."

"Their majesties have tried every-thing," said her father.

"Tell me again about the party to celebrate his birth," Serena said.

Once more, she heard the story about the four winds. She listened, nodding, then she said, "The cold came from the North Wind. I will go to the warm South Wind. She may be able to melt the ice."

Chapter Four

Serena and the South Wind

After many weeks onboard a sailing ship, Serena arrived at a tropical island. The sea was a clear blue, the sand pale gold, and palm trees sang the songs of the South Wind.

Beyond the palms, Serena came upon a garden that was a tangle of scented flowers. Jasmine flowers hung over arches and brushed against her face. Fountains splashed into ponds of pink and blue lotus flowers. Serena was standing, lost in wonder, when the

South Wind landed beside her in a shower of pink petals.

"You are looking for me?" the South Wind asked in a kindly voice.

Serena told her about Prince Tashka and the beautiful women who had wanted to marry him. "He deserves to be happy," she said.

"Ah, yes, that party!" said the South Wind. "I remember my sister's enormous sneeze. It was an accident, of course, but I can't undo it. It was the North Wind's sneeze. You'll have to talk to the North Wind."

"That means going to the North Pole," said Serena.

"Yes, my dear," said the South Wind. "But listen to my advice. At that party, we had gifts for the baby. You will need to use them."

"Those gifts belong to Prince Tashka," Serena replied. "They're kept in the royal treasure house."

"Borrow them," said the South Wind.

"Why?" asked Serena.

"The way is very difficult." The South Wind gave a sigh that brought down a fresh shower of petals. "You will not get to the North Pole without them."

Chapter Five

The Journey North

When Serena returned to the palace, she told her father about her meeting with the South Wind. Her father went to the king and queen, who were pleased that Serena was trying to help their son.

"Of course she must take the gifts," said the king. He packed a soft leather bag with the jeweled hummingbird, the golden music box, the emerald lamp, and the ivory whistle. He also gave Serena warm clothes and a strong gray horse to carry her. "Bring us good news," said the queen.

Serena rode north until the land turned white with snow, and icicles hung like white candles in the trees. When the snow became too deep for the horse, she unpacked her bags. "Go back home, good friend," she said. Then, with the bags on her back, she continued her journey on foot.

Each day became more difficult. There were mountains to climb, rivers of ice to cross. Sometimes, Serena wished that she could turn back like the horse. Then she thought of poor Prince Tashka. "To have no feeling is to be only half alive," she said to herself. "I am lonely. I am afraid. But those

feelings tell me that I am fully alive."

One morning, as Serena trudged across a white wasteland, she had a sense that she was being followed. She turned to see a great white bear behind her. It was on its hind legs, ready to attack.

Serena looked at the bear's claws and sharp yellow teeth. She put her hand in the leather bag and grabbed the ivory whistle. She put it to her lips, hoping that the noise would scare the bear. As the long claws came toward her, she blew a clear note.

Instantly the air became white with a blizzard. Snow whirled around her in a thick curtain, and the bear, unable to see, grunted and ran away.

Chapter Six

Serena and the North Wind

After the experience with the bear, Serena often used the gifts. Each morning she put the hummingbird around her neck. Instead of having to walk through knee-deep snow, she could fly like a bird and go much farther in a day's travel. At night, in caves, she went to sleep with music from the golden music box, while the light from the emerald lamp kept her warm. Several times, hungry wolves or bears came to her cave. As quick as a whistle, she could escape into her own snow storm.

At last Serena arrived at the North Pole. Like an exhausted bird she fell out of the sky, covered with feathers of snow. Before her was a tall castle of ice, the home of the North Wind. As she walked into the darkened courtyard, she held up the emerald lamp, and a thousand green lights shone like stars in the glassy walls.

A cold breeze caused the lamp to flutter. "Serena," whispered a voice, and there was the North Wind with long white hair and a gown that sparkled with silver snowflakes. "My sister told me you were coming."

"Please, North Wind," cried Serena,

her teeth chattering with cold. "I beg a great favor ..."

"I know why you are here," the North Wind replied. "I'm sorry. What is done is done, and I can't change it. But don't despair, my dear. There is hope. You already hold the gift that can solve the prince's problem." With that, there was a puff of snow and the North Wind disappeared.

At first, Serena felt great disappointment. But she was cheered by the thought that the answer lay with one of the gifts.

Wearily, she turned to begin the homeward journey.

Which one of the gifts would melt the ice in Prince Tashka's heart?

Chapter Seven

The Fifth Gift

Serena'a skin was burned with sun and snow. Her hair and clothes were ragged from travel. Without a thought for her appearance, she went straight to the palace and the prince.

"Where have you been, Serena?" the prince asked. "I haven't seen you for months."

Serena set the leather bag of gifts on a table. "Your highness, I have been seeking a cure for you."

"A cure? But I have no illness." The

prince looked at the bag, his eyes as clear and as cold as ice.

Serena went on. "These are the gifts you were given when you were born. I have reason to believe that one of them will melt your frozen heart. Then you'll be able to feel."

"Why should I want to feel?" he said. "It seems to me that all the war in the world is caused by feeling. People hate. People get angry."

"Yes, but people also love," said Serena. "They feel happiness. They laugh, and cry when they see beauty. Feelings make people truly alive."

The prince shrugged. "You don't convince me. I am sure emotion must be a great nuisance. I can live without it."

"Please, your highness," begged Serena. "Will you grant me a favor and hold this lamp?" She placed the emerald lamp in his hand and waited for the warm green glow to change him. Nothing happened. He handed the lamp back, "It is but a toy," he said.

She wondered if the answer was in the North Wind's gift, and she gave him the unicorn whistle. "Please, blow this, your highness."

As the prince blew, a whirling snow storm surrounded him. He stopped, and the snowflakes fell to his feet. "I have no use for this," he said, returning the whistle.

Next, Serena asked him to wear the hummingbird. As he put it around his

neck, his feet lifted off the ground and he flew once around the room. As he landed, he took off the necklace. "Serena, I told you, I am not interested in these things."

"There is one more," she said, giving him the golden music box.

As the sweet music filled the air, the prince yawned. "Take all these trinkets away," he said. He yawned again. "I do not want . . . I do not want . . ." He yawned. Then he lay back on his couch and fell fast asleep, the music box still in his hands.

Serena looked down at his cold, pale face. The gifts had not worked. His heart was still frozen. A flood of love and grief overwhelmed her, and her eyes filled with tears. Poor Prince Tashka! She blinked, and two large tears splashed onto the prince's linen shirt. Instantly, the tears spread and she saw that beneath the cloth, his heart was beating faster. A flush of color came to his cheeks. Then something wonderful happened. In his sleep, Prince Tashka smiled for the first time in his life.

For an hour, Serena sat beside the sleeping prince. Then gently, she closed the golden box, and the prince awoke. He sat up. His blue eyes shone with warmth and light. The ice in his heart had truly melted.

"Serena!" he cried. "I had a wonderful dream! The winter of my heart turned into spring, and I was walking in a

forest of flowers. My parents were there. I was so pleased to see them. I went farther, and in the middle of the forest, I discovered the woman I want to be my wife. At last, I know the meaning of happiness."

Serena smiled. She thought of all the beautiful women who had come to the palace. "Which one is she, your highness?"

"The one who is truly beautiful," he said, taking her hands in his.

"They are all beautiful," she said.

"But only one is truly beautiful. Only one loved me enough to risk her life for me. Only one had a heart big enough and warm enough to bring feeling to mine. That was the gift that cured me. Your love, Serena!"

Chapter Eight
Prince and Princess

Two years later, Prince Tashka and Princess Serena became the parents of beautiful twin daughters. What a celebration there was in the land! Bells rang. People danced in the streets. In the palace, the happy grandparents put on a huge party and everyone was invited.

The four winds blew in, dressed in their finest. One by one, they presented their gifts to the babies.

When it was the North Wind's turn,

she placed her presents some distance from the twin cribs, and all the time she kept her handkerchief over her mouth and nose, just in case she sneezed.